Game's Over
Life's Not

Game's Over Life's Not

The Athlete's Guide for Transitioning

Jonathan T. Orr

Game's Over Life's Not
Copyright © 2018

ISBN: 978-0-692-09648-2
LCCN: 2018903672

Published by Innorrvative Publishing
A division of Innorrvative LLC

Printed in the United States of America

Dedication

This book is dedicated to athletes who in their pursuit to achieve athletic greatness, forgot, or never realized that they were created for MORE! May this book serve as an inspiration and guide, helping you to discover your more.

Acknowledgements

I would like to extend a special thanks to Heydie Orr and Alison Fitzgerald for your labor of love in editing my manuscript. To Nicole Smith, thank you for sharing your gift of creativity to design the cover. Your support made this book possible. Thank you!

Contents

Chapter 1
U-Turn

"Identity issues were at the core of my struggles. After being an athlete for so long, I had subconsciously started to believe the lie, 'I am what I do'."

Chapter 1

I had made the drive up Evergreen Street to Henry Ford High School in Detroit, Michigan countless times before. Even after graduating from there seven years prior, I would still visit frequently when I came home on break from the University of Wisconsin, or during my off season as an NFL player. This day, like many other days in the past, I was returning at the request of a former teacher to speak to her classes about "success." Typically, during this drive I would be going over my message, thinking about my main points, and whether I should open with a joke. But not this day, this day was different.

This day I was bombarded with anxiety, fear, and embarrassment. The closer I got to the school the more intense my inner turmoil became. Thoughts raced through my head, "How will they perceive me now? What will they say? Do I have anything to offer anymore?" By the time I pulled into the parking lot, the thought came, "You're not a football player anymore; nobody will care about anything you have to say." Convinced this belief was true, I then made a U-turn in the parking lot and left the school. That day marked the beginning of a journey, a transitional journey that would be filled with doubt, confusion, reflection, self-discovery, and eventually triumph.

My journey over the next couple of years helped me to understand the root causes that led to me leaving that day, the feelings of inadequacy, as well as the other struggles I would face during my transition into life after football. Identity issues were at the core of my struggles. After being an athlete for so long, I had subconsciously started to believe the lie, "I am what I do." Somewhere in between the first time I strapped on a helmet for the Westside Broncos at nine-years-old, and the last time I strapped on a helmet for the Oakland Raiders, football had changed from being something I *did*, to being who I *was*. But I will talk more about that later.

Finding my purpose outside of being an athlete was another significant struggle I dealt with. Not only did I fail to realize who I was, but I also had no idea what I should do with my life. This was partly a by-product of not establishing an identity outside of being an athlete. Much of our purpose is closely related to our unique identity. Therefore, my one-dimensional sense of identity hindered me from tapping into my purpose outside of playing football.

The challenge of finding my purpose was also a result of a lack of preparation. For years, I had been intentional about preparing for many next seasons. To ensure that I would be successful during the football season, I would lift weights, condition, eat *(somewhat)* healthy, review film, and practice religiously. Unfortunately, I was not as intentional about preparing for my next season of *life*. But I will come back to this later also.

Since dealing with my struggles of transitioning into life after athletics, I have come to realize that I am not alone in this. During my transition and after, I witnessed former teammates wrestle with similar feelings and challenges. Severe issues with identity and struggles with finding purpose caused many of them to also make U-turns of their own.

A few years ago, I started Athlete Transition Services (ATS), an organization with a mission to help prepare athletes for life after sports. Through this work, I have had the opportunity to research, interview, and meet with thousands of former college and professional athletes. These are men and women from a variety of backgrounds, regions, races, sports, etc. In fact, the only common denominator is that each of them are former athletes who competed at high levels. One of the questions that we consistently ask these athletes is "What were the most challenging aspects associated with transitioning from sports into the next phase of life?" An overwhelming majority of their responses are connected to identity issues and struggling to find meaningful purpose.

Chances are that if you are reading this book you are a current athlete or a former athlete. Regardless of which category you fit, it is important to understand the potential struggles related to your transition into the next season of life, as your ability to successfully manage this transition is crucial to your health, growth, and overall success. This book was inspired by my personal experience, as well as the experiences of other athletes. My hope is that by reading this book you will be better prepared to successfully navigate through your personal transition into your next season of life.

Chapter 2
Preparing for the Transition
Process

"It is crucial to be aware of the transition process that accompanies no longer playing. Simply being aware of it significantly increases the likelihood that you will have a successful and healthy transition."

Chapter 2

Like many athletes, I knew one day there would be a change in my life in which I would no longer play football. However, like many athletes, I was completely oblivious to the fact that this change would be accompanied by a transition - one I was grossly unprepared for. Now, you may be asking yourself, "What's the difference between change and transition?" Let me explain, *change* is what happens to you. It is an external difference in your situation or circumstance. Usually, it is sudden. Although you may know the change is coming for a while, the moment or event that solidifies the change is quick.

A *transition*, on the other hand, is what happens to you internally as a product of the change you are faced with. Unlike change, transition takes time because it is an actual *process* that you go through. Transitional Management expert, William Bridges, stated that "Change is situational. Transition, on the other hand, is psychological. It is not those events, but rather the inner reorientation or self-redefinition that you have to go through in order to incorporate any of those changes into your life." (Bridges, 2004).

A good example of a change vs. transition was when Hillary, my sixth-grade girlfriend, broke up with me. We were together for nearly a month (which, by the way, constitutes a long-term relationship in middle school). Although the last week of our relationship consisted of multiple red flags - such as her avoiding me at lunch, giving me the silent treatment at recess, putting lines through my name that she had previously drawn hearts around, and rumors about her liking the new boy, Ryan - we were still together. One cold and rainy day, she approached me on the playground, accompanied by some of our friends (who by the way I am still angry with for not giving me a heads up) to tell me that it was officially over. That moment changed everything. Immediately, I no longer had a girlfriend, I was no longer someone's boyfriend. I was a single man again.

The change of no longer being in a relationship with Hillary was then followed by the process of transition. I had to deal with the anxiety of answering the "what happened?" questions. I worried about whether I would ever find such happiness again, I wrestled with the idea of not going to the Valentine's dance, and God forbid, seeing her dancing with Ryan to our song, Boyz II Men's *End of the Road*. See, I was faced with a change when Hillary broke up with me. I then navigated through the transition process because of the impact that change had on my thoughts and emotions.

William Bridges also suggests that for us to have a successful transition, we must properly navigate through three stages of the transition process. These stages are classified as the *ending, the neutral zone*, and the *new beginning*. The *ending* is the initial stage of transition when we first encounter the change. This stage is frequently accompanied with resistance and emotional turmoil, because we must let go of something that we are familiar and comfortable with. In this stage, you must accept the fact that your career has come to an end *before* you can begin to embrace your new life. Or in the case of my 6th grade break up, I had to come to terms with the fact that it was over and accept the fact that Hillary and I were not meant to be.

The second stage of the transitional process is the *neutral zone*, which is the link between the old and new. You might still be somewhat attached to the old while at the same time learning to adapt to your new way of life. This can be an uncomfortable time when you experience confusion, resentment, uncertainty, and impatience. It can be a state of limbo, where it is hard to find something to hold onto. The old way no longer works, yet the new way does not feel right either. You must use the neutral zone as an opportunity to reflect, explore, strategize, and focus on the future. Initially, after my breakup with Hillary I was upset and somewhat confused as to what happened and why. I soon realized that living in the past was holding me hostage and could cause me to miss out on future opportunities for love in middle school. So, I shifted my focus from the past into future possibilities.

After you successfully matriculate through the first two phases of the transitional process, you then arrive at the *new beginning*. The new beginning is a place of acceptance, hope, and comfort. In this place, you have learned to let go of the old and are now embracing the new. You have developed a level of comfort with the new changes in your life. Eventually, I arrived at a new beginning after my sixth-grade breakup. Although I did not have another girlfriend that school year, I became comfortable with being a bachelor and even enjoyed it. Sure, having a girlfriend was nice. But I learned that being single had its perks too-like not having to share my Hot Cheetos and being able to sit by whomever I wanted to on the bus.

As I mentioned earlier, I knew one day I would no longer play football, the *change*. But since I was clueless about the transition that would happen because of that change, I was not mentally or emotionally prepared. In fact, I did not even realize I was dealing with a transition process until years later. Consequently, I did not properly come to terms with the *ending* and had no sense of direction during the *neutral zone*, therefore delaying my arrival to my *new beginning*.

It is crucial to be aware of the transition process that accompanies no longer playing. Simply being aware of it significantly increases the likelihood that you will have a successful and healthy transition. Being aware allows you to prepare accordingly. It's no different than preparing for competition in sports. In most cases, you have experienced receiving some variation of a scouting report about upcoming opponents. This report included information about your opponent's strengths, weaknesses, tendencies, etc. By having this information, you became aware of what to expect and could prepare yourself to be successful during competition. Likewise, when you are aware of the transition process then you can prepare a game plan that will position you for success.

Chapter 3
Who Am I? – Wrestling with Identity Issues

"Since my identity was wrapped up in what I did, then it only made sense that once I was done playing football, I had no idea who I was. Because football no longer existed, I also ceased to exist, or so I thought."

Chapter 3

As I previously stated, identity issues were at the core of my challenges as well as most of the former athletes that I have worked with over the years. Before I could address my identity issues, it was first important for me to understand why I had them. I needed to figure out what was the root cause. Through prayer and self-reflection, I discovered that playing football had become who I *was* and not what *did*. The extent to which I identified myself was disproportionately tied to being an athlete. In other words, most, if not all my identity eggs, were in one basket - the athlete basket. As a result, I adopted an "I am what I do mindset," which ended up being the root cause for my identity struggles.

This unhealthy athletic identity had been slowly developing over the course of several years. A big reason for this was due to the societal pedestal athletes are often placed on in our culture. Like many athletes who have competed at high levels, I had been playing since I was very young. Because I was good at sports as a child, I started to receive recognition early on for it. As I got older, I became more successful in my athletic endeavors. Along with the success came more attention, praise, and even preferential treatment. Free food from the local restaurants, discounted shoes and clothes from the neighborhood mall, extra time to turn in assignments from teachers, and excessive attention and admiration from peers, were all things I had become accustom to by the time I finished high school. I was idolized simply because I could run fast and catch a football.

Being placed on such a pedestal conveyed to me the flawed messages of "I matter because people treat me this way," and, "I am treated this way because of what I do." Being treated a certain way for so long because I was an athlete led to blurred lines between who I was and what I did. Eventually it got to the point where the primary way I identified myself was as an *athlete*. I, like many athletes, started to believe the dangerous lie, "I am what I do." My identity, along with my sense of self-worth, self-respect, and self-confidence were all wrapped up in being a football player.

The "I am what I do" way of thinking is problematic for several reasons. Even prior to transitioning into life after football, this paradigm caused my self-worth, self-respect, and self-confidence to be based on my athletic performance. This false sense of identity was dangerous because my level of play on the football field dictated how I viewed and felt about myself. Thus, my self-perception suffered severely when I did not live up to my expectations or perform well on the field.

Another issue with this thought process is that no one plays forever. Since my identity was wrapped up in what I did, then it only made sense that once I was done playing football, I had no idea who I was. Because football no longer existed, I also ceased to exist, or so I thought.

Lastly, the "I am what I do" way of thinking is harmful because over time I subconsciously started believing that my athletic gifts

and abilities were all I had going for me. Because I was solely focusing on one of my God-given gifts for so long, I failed to recognize that I had more.

One of my former teammates also experienced this problem. He was, and still is, one of the most intelligent, focused, and overall positive individuals I know. Over the years we have known each other, I witnessed him work hard to accomplish goals he'd set and persevere after overcoming various obstacles on and off the field. He was a person I had come to have great respect for. A few years ago, I had the opportunity to visit him and hang out for a few days. During this time, he was on his second contract in the NFL. It did not take long for me to notice that his many years of playing football were starting to take a toll on him physically. He spoke of the aches and pains he felt in his knees and the complications he had using his hands at times. Everyday tasks, like getting out of bed, walking down the stairs, and getting in and out of the car were once easy for him but now had become quite challenging.

While sitting at his kitchen table one night, he confirmed what I already knew. He shared with me that he did not feel as though he could physically play any longer. He explained how the wear and tear he had sustained over the years was adding up and causing him serious health issues. After listening to him share this with me, I proposed that he seriously consider retirement. I told him, "You've had a pretty good career. You've accomplished a lot in this game and have done well for yourself financially. Maybe it is time to move on." I will never forget the words that came out of his mouth next.

With a straight face, he looked me in the eyes and said, "You're right, I know it's time to leave the game. But I can't. Football is all I know, the only thing I know how to do."

Hearing him say this was shocking and heartbreaking. I was shocked because I would have never imagined that he felt this way. Again, he is so intelligent, focused, and positive. If anyone could walk away from the game and be okay, it would be him. This broke my heart because I knew that what he believed was a lie. Football was not the only thing he was good at, and it was not the only thing he had going for himself. The "I am what I do" mindset had caused his identity and self-image to be distorted as he only viewed himself as a football player. Because he had solely focused on one of his God-given gifts for so long, he failed to recognize that he, too, also had more.

Chapter 4
Discovering Your True Identity

"Being an athlete is only one piece of who you are, and you are comprised of many other pieces. All of which are needed to complete your true, all-encompassing identity."

Chapter 4

Look at the can of soup below. Then, over the next 90 seconds, write down the ingredients that you believe are in this can on the lines below. Be sure to name as many as you can. Ready, set, go!

1. _____   11. _____
2. _____   12. _____
3. _____   13. _____
4. _____   14. _____
5. _____   15. _____
6. _____   16. _____
7. _____   17. _____
8. _____   18. _____
9. _____   19. _____
10. _____   20. _____

Hopefully, you were able to come up with a lot of ingredients. But, we will come back to this later. As established in the previous chapter, many athletes struggle with identity issues prior to, during, and after their transition. Although overcoming these issues can be challenging, it is not impossible. The first step is to know that you are more than just an athlete. Secondly, you must then redefine yourself. Lastly, you must take the time to acknowledge, embrace, and nurture the other aspects of your identity.

The first step in overcoming athletic identity issues is to know, I mean, *really* know, without a shadow of doubt that you are more than *just* an athlete. To do this, you must start to view yourself through a different set of lenses – lenses that will help you to look past your overrepresented athletic identity. By doing so, you will be able to see that being an athlete is only one piece of who you are, and you are comprised of many other pieces. All of which are needed to complete your true, all-encompassing identity.

You know the can of soup from earlier? I am pretty sure that regardless of how many ingredients you came up with, you did not name *any of* the following: beef, potatoes, green beans, peas, carrots, and celery. You may be thinking "All of that could not possibly be in that can because those typically are not ingredients included in tomato soup." Well, you are wrong. Beef, potatoes, green beans, peas, carrots, and celery are indeed inside of the can, along with many more ingredients. You see, what's inside of this can is actually vegetable beef soup. However, you did not name any of those ingredients because you were under the impression that the contents inside of the can were that of tomato soup because of the *label*. The label misled you into believing that all the can had to offer were the ingredients in tomato soup, but there is so much more on the inside of the can.

Athletes who struggle with identity issues are no different than the can of soup illustration. I was no different; I had placed, and allowed others to place, an "athlete only" label on me. I thought all I had to offer was my athletic gifts and talents. I assumed that running and catching were the ingredients that made up my identity because of the "athlete only" label that I saw when I looked in the mirror. It was not until I was able to look at myself with a new set of lenses that I could see that the "athlete only" label was an incomplete picture of who I truly was. That's when I was able to peel off the label and see what lied beneath - that before being an athlete, first and foremost, I am a human being. I am a person that was created with a range of natural talents, God-given gifts, and abilities, all of which make up my identity. As I did, you too must peel the label off and look within.

Once you have established that you are more than *just* an athlete, you must then redefine the foundation of your identity. Your identity can no longer be built on your athletic gifts and talents, it must be built on something solid and unwavering. You have to come to know the true essence of who you are at the core. For me to get to this place, I had to seek God and allow Him to reveal to me my true identity. In doing so, I came to realize that first and foremost, God made me a human being. That alone gives me all the innate worth, value, and respect I will ever need. There was nothing I had to do to earn it, nor is there anything I could do to lose it. This revelation was liberating for me and served as the new foundation for which my identity could be built upon. I went from identifying myself as just an athlete, to a person.

After realizing that you are more than just an athlete and redefining the foundation of your identity, it is then time to discover other aspects of your identity. Focusing primarily on your athletic identity for so long may have made you lose touch with the other parts of your identity that make you unique. You may even be unaware of the fact that you have other areas of interest and other things you are good at.

By the time my football career was over, I was 25 years old. Even though I was relatively young, I had spent the last 16 years (over half of my life) focusing on becoming the best football player

I could be. In doing so, I had very little time to do other things. For the last 16 years, every fall was spent playing football, every winter and spring was spent conditioning for football, and every summer was spent practicing for football. Due to the amount of time and attention I gave to football, I did not prioritize discovering other parts of my identity. Therefore, it was not until after I was done playing that I realized there are other things I enjoy doing just as much as playing football, and some of which I am pretty freaking good at too.

During my journey of self-exploration, I discovered that I had many gifts, talents, and skills that I had not been aware of such as creativity, speaking, writing, administration, even stand-up comedy. In upcoming chapters, you will have the opportunity to engage in self-exploration exercises. I strongly encourage you to take the time to complete these exercises as they will help you to expand your sense of identity and develop confidence in knowing that there is much more to you than just your athletic ability.

Chapter 5
What Now? - The Struggles
of Finding a New Purpose

"Your gifts and talents often serve as clues, pointing you in the direction that you should go and leading you to what you should be doing."

Chapter 5

Another common challenge for athletes after they're done playing is finding meaningful purpose. Or in other words, struggling to figure out what to do with your life. Identity issues, perceived lack of preparation and experience, and not knowing where to start, are often the reasons behind this struggle. If you have not addressed the identity issues discussed in the previous chapters, it may hinder your ability to find purpose in the next phase of your life. This is because your meaningful purpose is closely connected to the various gifts and talents contained within your identity. Your gifts and talents often serve as clues, pointing you in the direction that you should go. Thus, a lack of identity awareness creates a lack of understanding in your purpose outside of athletics.

A perceived lack of preparation and experience is another common hindrance for athletes in transition. You may be under the impression that you are not prepared for the "real world," or that your experiences in life thus far, especially as an athlete, are not related to your next season of life. Notice I did not call this hindrance a lack of preparation and experience, rather, a "perceived" lack of preparation and experience.

In my first attempt to find employment after football, I believed that my experience and preparation only provided me with options in the field of athletics. Even though I had absolutely no interest in becoming a coach, I asked a friend, Lee, to set up a meeting with the Athletic Director of a local school district in my area to discuss high school coaching opportunities. The meeting ended with the AD saying that I should expect a call from his office soon. Thankful, yet unenthused, I left the meeting with my friend. As we got off the elevator and headed for the exit sign, we crossed paths with the district's Assistant Superintendent of Student Services, who also happened to be a friend of Lee's. After the two gentlemen exchanged a handshake and hug, Lee made another introduction. "Meet my good friend Jonathan Orr. He is a recently retired professional football player and his currently looking for his next career opportunity." The Assistant Superintendent replied by saying, "Do me a favor Lee, don't take him anywhere else. I have room for him on my team." To make a long story short, in less than two weeks the Assistant Superintendent hired me.

A few months later, over burgers and fries one afternoon, I asked "Why did you hire me even though I had no experience?" He told me that being a former athlete himself, he knew that my experiences as an athlete had prepared me to be successful in life. He explained how he could teach me the specifics of the job duties, but things like a hard work ethic, dealing with success and failure, and understanding the importance of teamwork, he couldn't teach. "These are things learned from experience, and your experience as an athlete has taught you those things." The truth is that you are more than prepared for various opportunities and equipped with significant experiences that will serve you well as you move forward. You must first recognize your strengths before you can use them.

Another hurdle many athletes in transition wrestle with is confusion about where to start. You might be asking yourself questions like, "Should I go back to school? Should I pursue a career in the field I majored in? Should I take a job I was offered, even though I have no interest in it? Should I consider getting into coaching? Who should I talk to? Where should I live?" - and the list goes on. You may have numerous opportunities lined up. Or perhaps you may not have identified any opportunities at all. Either way, figuring out the first steps can be difficult and failure to do so may delay your transitional process, particularly at the neutral zone level. But don't worry, I'm not going to leave you hanging, in upcoming chapters we'll cover strategies that can help you figure out where to start.

Chapter 6
The Value and Power of Transferable Skills

"The same skills that have helped to make you a successful athlete can be transferred and utilized in various career fields, thus making you an asset to employers, and prepared for entrepreneurial opportunities."

Chapter 6

One advantage to being an athlete is that when your career is over you take some valuable things with you from your athletic experience. The trophies and awards you've acquired are one of the things that you take with you. These represent the various accomplishments you have achieved as a result of your hard work and commitment. Memories are another thing that will remain with you long after your days of competition are over. Memories of great wins, tough losses, overcoming adversity, traveling to different places, locker room shenanigans, and so on. You also have the wonderful opportunity to walk away with lifelong relationships. The bonds and trust that have been established between you, your teammates, and your coaches often extend beyond the seasons and can last for a lifetime.

Awards, memories, and relationships are no doubt valuable keepsakes that you have the privilege to take with you. However, there is another gift that you walk away with that is just as significant. I am talking about your gift of transferrable skills. Transferrable skills are skills that you have acquired from your vast participation in sports that can be utilized in other areas of your life and other career opportunities. Teamwork, performing under pressure, time management, setting goals, implementing a plan, and dealing with success as well as failure are just some of the many common transferrable skills that you possess.

Identifying and understanding your transferrable skills is crucial for your transition because it helps to dispel the myth that you are lacking preparation and experience. You have most likely been developing a unique set of skills since childhood and with each year of experience these skills have become more refined. The same skills that have helped to make you a successful athlete can be transferred and utilized in various career fields, thus making you an asset to employers and preparing you for entrepreneurial opportunities. However, if you are going to take advantage of your transferable skills you must first recognize that you have them, be able to articulate them, and then determine what opportunities you would like to pursue in which these skills will serve you well.

A great example of the value and power of an athlete's transferable skills can be seen in an experience my brother, Jeremy, had while in law school. Toward the end of Jeremy's first year of law school he went on an interview for a paid summer internship opportunity with one of the state's top environmental law firms. To say that paid internships for first year law students are competitive would be an understatement. One of the reasons they are so sought after is because they pay extremely well. In most cases the interns are compensated at the same rate as the new lawyers at the firm. Also, for interns who perform well, it is common for them to get invited back the following summer, and often the law firm will extend a job offer pending graduation and successful completion of the Bar Exam. Due to the limited spots available for these internships, roughly only 10% of first year law students are able to get one.

Within the first few minutes of the interview, Jeremy is sitting across from the law firm associate as he glances over his resume. The associate then looks up at Jeremy and says "Wow, so you played football and ran track at Michigan State University?" Jeremy answers the associate and says, "Yes, I was a two-sport athlete at MSU." The associate then explained to Jeremy how he was a Notre Dame Alumni and how he has always enjoyed the MSU and Notre Dame rivalry. For the next 45 minutes, all the associate did was engage Jeremy in dialogue about his experience as a college athlete and the great Notre Dame and MSU games over the years. There were no questions about Jeremy's GPA, the extracurricular activities and clubs he was involved in during his first year of law school, or his knowledge of environmental law as it related to the internship responsibilities. They only talked about sports.

After their sports conversation came to an end, the associate thanked Jeremy for applying and said, "Congratulations, I would like to offer the internship to you. When are you available to start?" Elated and a bit confused, Jeremy proceeded to thank the associate for the opportunity and answers his question. Before leaving the office, Jeremy said, "Would you like to know anything about what I have learned in law school so far or during grad school? I noticed we didn't really go over anything on my resume other than my athletic background. Do you have any questions for me?" The associate smiled at Jeremy and said, "You were a college athlete.

That tells me everything I need to know. You possess everything we are looking for. I know you are coachable, a team player, can meet deadlines, and can work well under pressure. You would be a great fit here." In other words, the associate recognized and valued the skills that Jeremy had developed from being an athlete and he knew those skills would transfer into Jeremy's role within their law firm. This is an illustration of the power and value of transferrable skills in action.

Transferable Skills Assessment

While doing this exercise, think about all of your experiences so far. Take note of the activities and responsibilities that have become a normal part of your life, especially athletics. These activities have offered you the opportunity to develop many of the skills listed below. Complete the first portion of this exercise by ranking yourself for each skill. Then complete the summary and action plan on the last page of this worksheet.

Well-developed - I have examples where I have done this in the past. I am confident that I can use this skill effectively when required.

Some experience - I have used this skill but would benefit from opportunities to develop this further.

Under-developed - I have not developed this skill or availed of opportunities where it may have been possible to do so.

People Skills	Well-Developed	Some Experience	Under-Developed
Team Work Skills - Openly expresses views and opinions within a group. Shows willingness to take on tasks and responsibilities to help the team reach its objectives.			
Communication Skills – Can speak clearly and listen attentively. Possesses the ability to convey information so it's received and understood, maintaining appropriate body language and clarifying where necessary.			

Presentation Skills – Can present information clearly and confidently to individuals and groups maintaining good eye contact, keeping attention while getting the desired message across.			
Leadership Skills – Can communicate a vision or goal to others and lead them towards achieving it. Pushes for action and results and wins the support of colleagues and team members.			
Interpersonal Skills – Relates well to people and can control feelings that emerge in difficult situations and respond appropriately.			
Influencing Skills – Shows ability to persuade people at all levels of an organization, easily wins co-operation and support for ideas or projects.			

Task Skills	Well-Developed	Some Experience	Under-Developed
Organization Skills – Effective use of resources to ensure that goals or projects are completed on time.			
Time Management – The ability to prioritize and use time efficiently to ensure that all relevant work is scheduled and completed in accordance with agreed timelines.			

Business Acumen – Understands the main business activities and strategic direction of their organization and keeps up with new developments in the field.			
Computer/Technical – Proficient in the use of basic computer packages and up to date with packages that are essential for your chosen career.			
Problem Solving – Identifying and evaluating issues or road blocks in a particular task and taking the necessary action to resolve them effectively.			

Personal Skills	**Well-Developed**	**Some Experience**	**Under-Developed**
Initiative – Not afraid to implement something new to new, seeks opportunities to influence make decisions.			
Learning – Open to learning new things and committed to personal development, seeks feedback to improve performance.			
Motivation – Driven to exceed at tasks, shows confidence in ability and expects to hit agreed targets.			
Integrity – Maintains confidential information and behaves professionally when dealing with colleagues and customers.			

Adaptability – Embraces new challenges and new ways of doing things. Not fazed by changing plans and able to react effectively to new ideas and targets.			

Transferrable Skills Summary and Action Plan

Based on your responses to the self-assessment you should now take note of the skills that are your strengths and that you would mention in cover letters and be prepared to discuss at interviews. Employers often ask questions about your strengths during interviews. In order to prepare for this, make a note of what you believe are your top three skills with examples of where you developed them in the box below.

Top three skills (including examples of where I have developed them)

1._____
_____
_____
_____
_____

2._____
_____
_____
_____
_____

3._____
_____
_____

_____

_____

Now you should reflect on the skills that you feel you need to develop that may be essential for the career area you are interested in. In the space provided below identify three skills that you feel you should try to develop in the near future. Also think about opportunities that would help you to do so.

Skills I need to develop (including examples of activities that will help you develop them)

1._____

_____

_____

_____

_____

2._____

_____

_____

_____

_____

3._____

_____

_____

_____

_____

Adapted from Basingstoke Job Clubs
(https://basingstokejobclubs.wikispaces.com/)

Chapter 7
Start with Your Head and Heart

"When you are doing things that you are passionate about and good at, as opposed to things that you don't really care about and are not so good at, it satisfies you holistically."

Chapter 7

Earlier in Chapter 5 I mentioned that one of the reasons athletes in transition struggle with finding meaningful purpose after they're done playing is a result of not knowing where to start. Whether you are presented with multiple opportunities or you must seek out opportunities, it can be challenging when it comes to deciding which route to pursue. One of the best things you can do to successfully handle the challenge of figuring out where to start is to identify what is in your *heart*.

By heart, I am referring to your passion. I am talking about the groups of people, places, things, or issues that give you life! The things in your heart that move you. It could be something that brings you significant joy or something that makes you angry to the point of taking action. When you ask yourself, "What do I do with my life now?" the next question you should ask is "What do I care about? "The answers to the second question will provide insight on how to answer the first question.

You may be like many of the athletes I have worked with over the years who are having trouble identifying what is in their heart. As you think about it, your initial response might be "I am passionate about my sport." Although this may indeed be a true statement, it is vital that you understand and are able to identify the *rest* of what you care about. Once you can spend some time reflecting on this, you can think about your life in a broader sense and identify your other passions. You may start to realize that you love working with children who have special needs, or that gang violence infuriates you, or that you become overjoyed at the thought of starting a business. It is important for you to understand that just because the passions in your heart might be hard to identity at first, it does not mean that they are not there. You may have been solely focused on your athletic passion for such a long time that your other passions have been lying dormant and must be awakened.

Retired five-time NBA Champion, Kobe Bryant has transitioned exceptionally well, especially as it relates to finding purpose outside of basketball. During an interview on ESPN's *First Take*, Bryant recommends that players start thinking about their purpose outside of the game sooner rather than later. "For the young guys coming up, as you're going through your career it's important that you start looking for things that you're equally as passionate about," Bryant continued, "Because when the music stops, and the game is over and you're just trying to figure it out after...you're already too late." (Bryant, 2017).

When asked about not missing basketball Bryant stated, "I know it's strange, but it's a blessing, you grow up playing the game your whole life, and this is what you identify yourself with the whole time, it's very hard to find something else. You know, I've been very fortunate, very blessed to have a passion I love every bit as much as playing basketball." (Bryant, 2017).

In addition to figuring out what's in your heart, it is also important for you to start with your head as well. By head, I mean the things that come easily to you and that you are naturally good at.

These may be things that you can do almost effortlessly. The heart tells you the area you should work in, but the head provides insight as to what you should be doing in that area.

Like the heart, you may struggle with identifying what's in your head too. Again, for so many years you might have been primarily focusing on one dimension of your talents. Thus, neglecting to recognize and utilize your other gifts. However, after engaging in self-reflection in which you contemplate questions like, "What do I enjoy doing for long periods of time? What do people consider me an expert in? What would I enjoy doing at work even if I did not get paid for it? What am I very knowledgeable about?" - you will be able to discover your other gifts, talents, and skills outside of being an athlete.

After you have identified what's in your heart and your head you should then pursue career opportunities that would allow you to incorporate both. When you are doing things that you are passionate about and good at, as opposed to things that you don't really care about and are not so good at, it satisfies you holistically. When you operate in this space, chances are you're fulfilling your life's purpose and using your God-given gifts at the same time. You are more likely to be successful and enjoy your work because your endeavors become meaningful and not just a means to an end.

A few years ago, I took a job with a non-profit organization whose mission aligned with my heart. I was very passionate about the people and the community that the organization served. However, most of my job duties did not align with my head. I was responsible for conducting healthcare law research and determining the implications these laws would have on our organization. I was also tasked with the duty of creating our monthly budget reports. Roughly 75%-80% of my time was spent behind a desk looking at a computer screen. The issue was that my job duties did not align with talents, gifts, or skill-set. Sure, I was able to adapt and learn how to do these things, but the work was still dreadful and boring. It only took me a few months before I was burned out.

After being with the organization for nearly a year, I was presented with an opportunity to change positions. The new position would provide me an opportunity to utilize what was in my head. Some of the job duties included coordinating events, fundraising, public speaking, and establishing partnerships. Needless to say, I changed positions and the remainder of my time with the organization was one of the best professional experiences of my life because I was able to do something I was passionate about and good at. If you are wrestling with the question "What do I do with my life now?" a great place to start is with your head and your heart.

Heart and Head Self-Discovery Exercise

Take two minutes and write down as many "Heart" items that come to mind. Remember, your "Heart" is the people places and things you are passionate about. These are the topics and issues that move you. These are things you are deeply connected and drawn to, things that make your heart beat faster, because you find them captivating, extremely irritating, or exhilarating.

Then take two additional minutes and write down as many "Head" ideas that come to mind. Remember, your "Head" is the things you are good at. These are your special talents: the skill-sets, unique abilities, insights, and everything else that you have to offer. This also includes the knowledge obtained from past experiences, and your connections to people and places that others may not have.

Heart	Head

Chapter 8
Clarifying Your Work-Related Values

"Although money is an important factor to consider, it should not be the driving force in your career decisions. Taking the time to clarify and prioritize your work-related values will help you to put money in its rightful place of factors when considering career opportunities."

Chapter 8

The next step in figuring out what to do with your life, after you have identified what you care about and what you're good at, is to clarify your work-related values. Work-related values are your must-haves in a job. These are the different factors in a job that are important to you. Even though an opportunity may correspond with your passion and strengths, you also need to make sure it is in line with your values as well. Some examples of work-related values include flexibility, day-shifts, opportunities for growth, healthcare benefits, salary, a laid-back culture, and autonomy.

Clarifying your values on the front end is important because it helps to simplify your decision-making process. If you are at the beginning stage of your job search or at the point of choosing between a few different job offers, knowing what work-related values are important to you can help you weed out the prospects that are not a good fit. If healthcare benefits are essential for you, and you find out that an opportunity you are considering as an independent contractor does not include healthcare benefits, then you might strongly consider eliminating that job from your list. But if you have not taken the time to identity your values then you might take the job, only to realize after the fact that it's lacking something that is of high importance to you.

In addition to clarifying your work-related values it is also important to prioritize them. You may identify ten values. Most likely, each of them will not be of equal importance to you. Half of the ten values might fall under "this would be nice to have, "whereas the remaining five might be "absolute must haves." Prioritizing your values can also help to simplify the decision-making process even more. It allows you to weigh competing opportunities in a more objective manner. There are various ways to prioritize values. Some people place them into categories such as *Very Important, Important*, and *Somewhat Important*. Whereas others rank them on a scale from 1 to 10. Whichever method you decide on for prioritizing your values is fine, as long as they get prioritized.

Clarifying your values will also help you to avoid making the common mistake of pursuing opportunities solely based upon how much money you will make. Although money is an important factor to consider, it should not be the driving force in your career decisions. Taking the time to clarify and prioritize your work-related values will help you to put money in its rightful place of factors when considering career opportunities. Not doing so may lead to the typical human default action of chasing after the biggest check, only to discover that money apart from meaningful purpose will leave you unfulfilled.

The same way that settling for a job that does not align with your heart and head can take away from having a positive work experience, so can failure to engage in work that accommodates your values. Again, your work-related values are things that you need, and if your needs are not being met the more likely it is that your level of job satisfaction will suffer, which will ultimately lead to discontent and burn out. To help prevent this from happening, view your various career opportunities as puzzles. You want to look for the puzzle in which all of your heart, head, and value pieces are included. The more of your pieces an opportunity encompasses, the more positive, complete, and fulfilling your work experience will be.

You may be asking yourself, "What if I am not finding career opportunities that fulfill my heart, head, and values?" In these instances, I would suggest two things; 1) choose the lesser of the evils, or, 2) create your own opportunity. When facing a situation in which your dream job is not an option, you and your circumstances dictate the immediate need for employment, and it is best to prioritize based on need. A great alternative to this strategy would be to create your own opportunity that will incorporate your heart, head, and values. Perhaps it's starting a business, a non-profit, a community program, or the pursuit of an educational path that aligns with where you want to go. In most cases this path will be harder, uncomfortable, and less predictable, but if done right it will be far more rewarding. Even if you must choose a lesser of the evils job but are still able to create your own opportunity simultaneously, then it provides you with hope that you are not stuck in your current situation.

Work-Related Values Assessment

Part 1: Underline all the values that are important in your work life over the next few years. Then narrow down your underlined list by circling the ten values that are most important to you.

Work Content	Work Environment	Work Relationships	Intrinsic Values
autonomy	job security	respectful	fulfilling
intellectually	flexibility	teamwork	integrity
stimulating	deadline	trust	status
leading	pressure	cultural identity	achievement
data driven	surroundings	caring	responsibility
expertise	income	competition	power
risk	action-oriented	cooperation	influence
innovating	diversity	privacy	appreciation
detail-oriented	structure	diversity	helping
meaningful	relaxed pace	collaboration	belonging
learning	casual	humor	independence
high standards	quiet	peaceful	contributing
focus	structured	autonomy	service oriented
creativity	excitement	recognition	authenticity
variety	pressure	support	commitment
growth	predictability	open	honesty
knowledge	location	communication	having an
control	work w/ public	people contact	impact
exciting	comfortable	independence	fairness
helping	balance	fun	work quality
outcomes	equality	professionalism	goal-oriented
other:	other:	other:	other:

55

Part 2: Circle your top five core values out of the ten that you previously underlined. These are the values that you absolutely must have at work. List your five core values in the space provided below in order from most important to least important.

My Top 5 Core Values

1._____

2._____

3._____

4._____

5._____

Chapter 9
Use Your GPS
(Goal + Plan = Success)

"After setting your goal, the next step is to develop a plan for reaching it. The plan is important because it helps to identify the practical actions needed to reach your goal. Without a plan, a goal is merely a wish."

Chapter 9

After you have recognized the power and value of your transferrable skills, identified what's in your heart and head, and clarified your work-related goals, it is then time to use your GPS. No, I am not referring to the device on your phone or in your vehicle that helps you travel from point A to point B. Instead, I am referring to a formula that can be used to help you navigate through your transition and achieve success. The formula is Goal + Plan = Success. The first step is to set a professional or educational goal for your transition that is based on what you've discovered about your passion, strengths, skills, and values. Then you want to formulate a corresponding plan that will assist you in achieving your goal. These first two steps will lead you to success. I understand that there are many different definitions of success. But for the sake of this formula, we will define success as arriving at your desired next level or reaching the goal you set.

In addition to making sure your goal is in line with your passion, strengths, skills, and values, you also want to make sure that you set a S.M.A.R.T goal. S.M.A.R.T stands for *Specific, Measurable, Achievable, Relevant,* and *Timely* goals. *Specific* means that the goal should be very detailed, not vague. For example, instead of "I would like to further my education," a more specific goal would be "I will earn a Master's Degree in Business Administration." *Measurable* means that there must be a way to know when the goal is accomplished. In the example above, the goal is measurable because

a degree will either be earned or not. *Achievable* means that the goal can realistically be accomplished with effort and commitment. In this case, when determining if earning an MBA is achievable, a person should consider factors like their time, schedule, and financial resources. *Relevant* means that the goal should have significance. In other words, earning an MBA must be important; there should be a motivating factor behind the goal. Timely means that there is a target date of completion for the goal.

After setting your goal, the next step is to develop a plan for reaching it. The plan is important because it helps to identify the practical actions needed to reach your goal. Without a plan, a goal is merely a wish. Your plan should be broken down into various action steps with target dates for each one. As you tackle each action step it will bring you closer to reaching your goal. In your plan, you should also account for any potential obstacles that you can foresee and the solutions for overcoming those obstacles. By thinking about the potential problems ahead of time, you will be better prepared to handle them more effectively and efficiently.

The strategy for setting your goal and implementation of a plan to help you successfully accomplish it is probably familiar to you. You may not have referred to it as GPS, but in one way or another it is a process that you have used numerous times as an athlete. During the off-season, you may have set goals to get stronger or to gain or lose weight. Prior to the start of each season you probably set individual or team goals such as setting personal records or winning your conference championship. Whether it was off-season goals or pre-season goals, the point of setting them was to provide you a focal point to work toward that would eventually get you to where you wanted to be.

However, setting the goal was not enough. It was just the starting point. To achieve your goal, you developed a plan that would give you the best opportunity to be successful in accomplishing your goal. If your goal was to lose weight, then your plan probably included a certain workout regimen and diet that guided your actions as you worked toward your goal. As you transition into life after athletics it is important to continue to utilize the goal-setting and planning process. Instead of setting goals for the next season in your sport, you'll be setting goals for your next season of life.

S.M.A.R.T Goal Tracker

Today's Date: _____ Target Date: _____ Start Date: _____

Date Achieved: _____

Goal:

_____

_____

Verify that your goal is SMART

Specific: *What exactly will you accomplish?*

_____

_____

_____

Measurable: *How will you know when you have reached this goal?*

_____

_____

_____

Achievable: *Is achieving this goal realistic with effort and commitment? Have you got the resources to achieve this goal? If not, how will you get them?*

_____

_____

_____

Relevant: *Why is this goal significant to your life?*

_____

_____

_____

Timely: *When will you achieve this goal?*

_____

_____

_____

Potential Obstacles	Potential Solutions
_____	_____
_____	_____
_____	_____
_____	_____
_____	_____
_____	_____
_____	_____

Who are the people you will ask to help you?

_____

_____

_____

Specific Action Steps: *What steps need to be taken to get you to your goal?*

What?	Expected Completion Date	Completed Date
_____	_____	_____
_____	_____	_____
_____	_____	_____
_____	_____	_____
_____	_____	_____

Chapter 10
The New Beginning

"I decided that I wanted to pursue a career path that would allow me to utilize my athletic background, professional experiences, education, heart, head, and values. That is how Athlete Transition Service Corp. was born."

Chapter 10

I started off this book by sharing the story about my U-Turn. Although that was a difficult moment in my life, as I look back on it, I am thankful for it. That moment of weakness and vulnerability initiated a process that allowed me to see the issues of my heart and wrestle with them. I was able to see that my identity was primarily wrapped up in what I did on the football field. Realizing this was an inaccurate assumption, I was then able to wrestle with the question of "Who am I," until I discovered my true identity. I was also able to recognize another lie that I believed, which was that my purpose in life began and ended with football. Realizing that this too was false, I then wrestled with the question, "What do I do now?" until I was able to walk in my new and meaningful purpose.

Today, that U-Turn also represents the road that led me to a new beginning. A new place of peace, hope, and fulfillment. Peace from knowing who I am and knowing that it is not defined by what I *do*. Hope in understanding that I have the rest of my life to look forward to, and that although this great part of my life as an athlete is over, there are still great things to come. Fulfillment from being able to use my other gifts, talents, and skills in a meaningful way, and in areas I am passionate about.

Since my U-Turn experience, I have been on quite an exciting personal and professional journey. My wife, Heydie, proudly (and sarcastically) says she has never met anyone who wears as many "hats" as I do. I haven't been afraid to dive into my heart in search of the "rest" of me. I have explored several of my other passions, such as teaching, mentoring, comedy, music, and writing through my career choices, hobbies, and entrepreneurship. And most importantly, since facing and overcoming my transition struggles, I have been able to support and encourage other people that have experienced similar challenges along the way.

Professionally, I have been on a path that started off in working with at-risk students as a Behavior Specialist in the Metropolitan Nashville Public School District. I was then able to use my leadership skills in an administrative role, as the Coordinator of School Safety for the district. While fulfilling these duties, I realized that I had a strong desire to continue to serve in a leadership capacity as I progressed in my career. This led to me attend Trevecca Nazarene University, where I earned a Master's Degree in Organizational Leadership. During this time, our family relocated from Tennessee to Michigan, after I was presented with an opportunity to return to my hometown, and utilize my education, skills, and gifts to serve the people of Detroit as the Executive Administrative of Finance and Operations and Director of Special Programs for The Salvation Army.

While in graduate school, I decided that I wanted to pursue a career path that would allow me to utilize my athletic background, professional experiences, education, heart, head, and values. That is how Athlete Transition Service Corp. (ATS) was born. The ATS organization is committed to helping athletes prepare for their transition into their next season of life. Through workshops and life coaching services, we facilitate the overall growth and development of athletes and empower them with the knowledge and strategies needed to have a successful and healthy transition. Prior to starting ATS, people would ask me a question that I did not have an answer to: "If money was not an issue, what could you see yourself doing every day for the rest of your life without getting paid for it?" ATS has now given me an answer to that question.

It is my sincere hope that you are successful in your transition into your next season of life. Whether you are in the midst of your transition right now or if it is a few years down the road, it is imperative to keep some things in mind. First, you must know that you are more than just an athlete - your identity is not synonymous with what you do. Secondly, you must know that you have a meaningful purpose outside of your athletic ability and it's time to discover it. Thirdly, remember that you are equipped with the power and value of transferrable skills. Fourth, be intentional about taking the time to discover your heart, head, and work values. Lastly, be sure to use your GPS to help you get to a place where your heart, head, and values intersect. By focusing on these areas, I am confident that you will arrive at your new beginning and declare that even though the game's over, life's not.

About the Author

Jonathan Orr was born and raised in Detroit, Michigan. At a young age, Jonathan's parents introduced him and his two brothers to the world of sports. It did not take long before Jonathan fell in love with athletics, especially football. By the time Jonathan was nine years old he had a goal to become a professional football player when he grew up.

Jonathan earned a football scholarship to the University of Wisconsin. During his time at UW, Jonathan earned a Bachelor's Degree in Community Leadership and Non-Profit Management. While at Wisconsin, Jonathan also found success on the football field, which led to him being drafted by the Tennessee Titans. His time in the NFL was short lived, lasting only two seasons before being released by the Oakland Raiders.

Shortly after the end of his football career, Jonathan found himself facing significant personal struggles. He did not know who he was without football or what to do with his life. Eventually, Jonathan developed a plan for transitioning into the next season of his life. This plan included utilizing the transferrable skills and strengths he had acquired from his athletic experiences, identifying his gifts and talents, and setting value-based goals. In just a few months, Orr had landed his first post-football career opportunity in the educational sector. A few years later, Jonathan earned his Master's Degree in Organizational Leadership from Trevecca

Nazarene University and has since worked in positions of leadership for various non-profit and educational organizations.

In 2014, Jonathan started Athlete Transition Services Corp., an organization that helps athletes prepare for life after sports. Through workshops and life coaching services, Jonathan and his team educate and equip athletes with the information, tools, and strategies needed to facilitate their overall growth and development. Jonathan has experienced a great deal of personal and professional success and it is his passion to help other athletes do the same. Currently, Jonathan resides in Canton, Michigan with his wife, Heydie and their children Carsyn, Catheryn, and Owen.

CONNECT WITH JONATHAN

For speaking engagements, workshops, interviews, life coaching or other requests send an email to:

INFO@ATSCORP.ORG

You can also follow Jonathan on social media:

@JORR_ATS

WORKSHOPS

Next Season Transition Workshop

Freshmen and Rookies in Transition

Money Management 101 for Athletes

Athleaders

Whole Health for Athletes

Addressing Identity Issues in Athletics

W.I.N in the Classroom

For more information about these workshops and

additional services please visit:

WWW.ATSCORP.ORG

WORKSHOP TESTIMONIALS

"When identifying professionals to bring in for our student-athletes, it is so imperative for that individual to be engaging, dynamic, and impactful. Athlete Transition Services provided exactly that. Jonathan and Jeremy delivered valuable knowledge and insight to our senior student-athletes as they prepare for the transition to the real world. This conversation has been a focus for our seniors and the Next Season workshop continued the conversation by helping our student-athletes gain understanding and confidence in their identity, as well as finding purpose in their personal pursuits."

Jessie Gardner
Director of Student-Athlete Enhancement
University of Alabama

"Jonathan has done it again! We have brought him back to Clemson for the third time to present on the Next Season Transition Workshop. He continues to improve adding fresh ideas from one year to the next ensuring relevancy in his delivery. The Next Season Transition Workshop provides something tangible for athletes to use as a resource during their transition, as well as a reminder of the many marketable qualities and skills athletes have mastered throughout their collegiate career. I would highly recommend bringing Jonathan and ATS to your campus. The passion he has for changing the lives of young adults is moving."

Kyra Lobbins
Director of President's Leadership and Strategic Initiatives
Clemson University

"Jonathan provided his Next Season workshop for our student athletes and it was very well received. Our student athletes appreciated his personal stories and examples of how he experienced the transition into life. Jonathan has advanced skills in relating to student athletes and making them reflect on their identity and what sets them apart from other college students when it's time to secure employment after college. We really appreciated Jonathan's attention to detail, organizational skills, and timeliness in coming in and staying within the time limits we had for our student athletes insofar as his workshop was on a school night and during a time in which many would be studying."

Dr. Jonathan Ravarino
Director of Psychology and Wellness
University of Utah

"We were excited to welcome Jonathan Orr back to UNO for his Next Season Transition and Money Management 101 workshops. His unique presentation regarding planning for the "next season", was totally in line with our goals of preparing our student-athletes for life after sports and graduation. Jonathan is rather relatable as a former student-athlete himself and was able to engage the audience because of his own personal experiences and storytelling ability. In addition, student-athletes can always use an extra reminder of how to successfully manage their finances, so the Money Management 101 was extremely relevant and needed by all. I am so thankful that Jonathan shared his message with our student-athletes and will highly recommend him to other campuses. We look forward to continuing our relationship with ATS and bringing them back to UNO for many years to come."

Kirsten Elleby
SWA / Assistant AD of Student Athlete Enrichment
University of New Orleans

"I'd like to thank Jonathan and Jeremy for taking the time to come to BGSU to discuss the process of transitioning to life after sport with our athletes. So many times we witness student athletes that go through identity issues after they exhaust their eligibility because as student athletes we demand so much out of them and they are truly committed to being the best they can possibly be in their sport. By doing this, they sometimes lose sight of who they are on the inside, as well as what career aspirations they may have outside of their sport. Athlete Transition Services provided a wake-up call to many of our athletes to look at themselves intrinsically to find what makes them tick and what they truly want from their educational experience. I would highly recommend ATS to come to your campus if you want your students to engage in a workshop that is interactive and causes a higher and deeper level of thinking by your students."

Chet Hesson
Assistant AD for Academics & Student Services
Bowling Green State University

"Jonathan's Money Management 101 presentation was a perfect fit for Virginia Tech student-athletes. Jonathan's experience as a student-athlete allowed him to connect easily and quickly with our students. He did a fantastic job relating lifelong financial concepts in an accessible way – a way that was not difficult for students to grasp yet the content was deep enough to benefit them for a lifetime. It is his genuine care and concern for student-athletes, however, that sets Jonathan apart. An audience can easily tell if a speaker sincerely cares about their actual well-being; Jonathan certainly does."

Danny White
Assistant AD of Student-Athlete Development
Virginia Tech

"Jonathan's ability to connect with his audience is truly unmatched. By taking a complex topic like financial literacy and making it engage, fun, and thought-provoking for SAs to ask questions and be empowered by the information he shared. I give Jonathan my highest recommendation."

Ashton Henderson
Associate Director of Football Academic Services / Seminole Leadership Program Coordinator
Florida State University

"Jonathan delivered his story with such grace and humor allowing him to relate and connect to the student-athletes. The workshop delivered valuable content and challenged the student-athletes to think about their values, transferable skills, and goals. I received great feedback from all that attended the workshop. Jonathan also provided a familiar face for our football student-athletes to look to and lean on. In this era of educating student-athletes on the importance of life after sport, I feel we do an injustice in providing our ethnic minority student-athletes with mentors that look like them. This was a great opportunity for all parties involved, and we were blessed to have Jonathan visit our campus. I highly recommend Jonathan to other universities, so he can share his story, and impact the lives of other student-athletes."

Amanda Pulido
Life Skills Coordinator
University of the Incarnate Word

"Jonathan delivers a thoughtful and important message on financial literacy with deft, humor, and astute understanding of the issue. His real-life examples, as well as the hands-on participation pieces, make it a subject that has staying power with his audience. I recommend him highly to present this topic to student-athlete populations."

Dr. Greg Beaumont
Associate Dean / Senior Associate AD
Florida State University

"Jonathan Orr's Next Season Workshop was jammed packed with thought-provoking concepts and activities that helped our student-athletes. Prior to the workshop, we discussed the topic and he was able to critique the presentation to fit our student-athletes at the DII level. The athletes were engaged throughout the entire presentation because he is interactive. He was relatable and spoke to the athletes at a level they could understand. We were pleased with his presentation and content. He provides an invaluable service to student-athletes. Helping student-athletes understand the transition process and finding an identity outside of sport is an obstacle very few are willing to engage. Thank you, Athlete Transition Services for tackling this issue."

Brandon Wright
Director of Career Services
Arkansas Tech University

For more testimonials please visit:

WWW.ATSCORP.ORG

References

Bridges, W. (2004). *Transitions: making sense of life's changes. 2nd ed.*, updated and expanded, 1st Da Capo Press ed. Cambridge, MA: Da Capo Press.

Bryant, K. [ESPN]. (2017, March 27). *Kobe Bryant Joins First Take* [Video file]. Retrieved from https://www.youtube.com/watch?v=o_gACZHOXAk

69742532R00046

Made in the USA
Middletown, DE
23 September 2019